THE LITTLE FLOWERS
* * * OF * * *
Saint Francis of Assisi

TRANSLATED BY
ABBY LANGDON ALGER

EDITED BY
LOUISE BACHELDER

ILLUSTRATED BY
VALENTI ANGELO

THE PETER PAUPER PRESS
Mount Vernon · New York

Preface

S AINT FRANCIS was born in 1182, in the little town of Assisi, in Umbria. His mother, Madonna Pica, was of noble race, and his father, Peter Bernardone, was a rich merchant, who was traveling in France on business at the time Francis was born. His mother was ill for many days until, by the advice of a pilgrim, she was laid on a bed of straw in a stable. Thus began that likeness between the life of Francis and that of Christ. Madonna Pica named her child John, in memory of the beloved disciple; but on his father's return with rich profits, he chose to call him Francis, for the country where he had been so successful.

The boy was taught by parish priests, and learned easily all that was taught him, showing an especial talent for the language of the land from which he took his name. He was foremost in the gayeties of the town, winning the sobriquet of the "flower of youth." So elegant were his tastes, that his parents often said, "He is more like the son of a prince than like our son." Still, they were proud of his splendor, and grudged him nothing, though his charities were as lavish as his pleasures: no beggar ever asked of him in vain.

When he had reached the age of twenty-four however, a war broke out between Assisi and

Perugia. Francis was taken prisoner, and for a year languished in captivity. Returning home, he suffered from a tedious illness which proved a turning-point in his career. He began to long for something better and higher than mere amusement. It was the age of knighthood, and his first thought was to redress wrong and help the weak. He began to devote himself more entirely to the sick and poor, particularly the lepers, of whom there were many at that time.

In the course of two years he restored three churches and gained twelve disciples, the first being Bernard of Quintavalle. Within eleven years these twelve grew to more than five thousand. The Franciscan Friars were vowed to abject poverty, owning absolutely nothing, thus differing from the other ecclesiastical bodies then in existence.

Francis next founded the Order of Poor Ladies, afterwards known as the Poor Clares, in honor of their first abbess, Clara Sciffi, a beautiful heiress, who left her home at the age of fifteen to enter upon a religious life. Later still the Third Order was established, which was open to men and women alike, and meant for those who lived in the world. These three Orders spread rapidly throughout the globe.

After enduring every privation and sorrow for many years, as well as many nameless raptures in his spiritual intercourse with God, he saw, as he prayed upon a lonely mountain, a vision of Christ crucified; and as he gazed, his body became stamped with the Stigmata, or marks of the passion of our Lord, which he thenceforth bore until his death, some two years after, October 4, 1226, in his forty-fifth year.

The chief quality of Saint Francis — the central and characteristic charm which has made him perhaps the best beloved of all the illustrious members of the calendar — is the depth and tenderness of his kind heart. The objects of his intense and exuberant love were not only God, angels, and men, but also animals, birds, insects, and even inanimate objects, which he was wont to address as his brothers and sisters. Many charming instances of his friendships with them may be found in these "Little Flowers."

The *Little Flowers* is a series of legends which were collected some two hundred years after his death, having been handed down by word of mouth until that time. The *naïveté* and antique flavor of the original text have been preserved in the present version of the legends selected for this edition.

A Simple Prayer

Lord, make me an instrument of Thy peace:
Where there is hatred, let me sow love;
Where there is injury, pardon;
Where there is discord, union;
Where there is doubt, faith;
Where there is despair, hope;
Where there is darkness, light!

O Divine Master, grant that I may not so
    much seek
To be consoled, as to console;
To be understood, as to understand;
To be loved, as to love;
For it is in giving that we receive,
It is in pardoning that we are pardoned,
And it is in dying that we are born
To Eternal Life.

SAINT FRANCIS OF ASSISI

Chapter One

IN THIS BOOK ARE CONTAINED CERTAIN LITTLE
FLOWERS, MIRACLES, AND DEVOUT EXAMPLES
OF THAT GLORIOUS POOR FOLLOWER OF CHRIST,
SAINT FRANCIS, AND OF CERTAIN OF HIS HOLY
COMPANIONS. TOLD TO THE PRAISE OF JESUS
CHRIST. AMEN.

WE HAVE first to consider that the glorious
Saint Francis was like unto Christ, our
blessed Lord; for even as Christ in the begin-
ning of His preaching chose to Himself twelve
Apostles who should renounce all worldly
things and follow after Him in poverty and in
other virtuous deeds, even so did Saint Francis.
Also even as one of the twelve Apostles of
Christ, reproved of God, went out and hanged
himself by the neck, so one of the twelve companions of Saint Francis, the same which was
called Brother John of the Chapel, did turn
apostate, and finally go out and hang himself
by the neck. And this is a worthy example for
the elect, and a subject for fear and humility,
considering that none can be sure of continuing
unto the end in the grace of God. And as those
holy Apostles were a wonder to all men for their
sanctity and humility, and were filled full with
the Holy Ghost, so too were the most holy companions of Saint Francis. A certain one among
them was snatched up into the third Heaven,

7

like Saint Paul, and that was Brother Guy; a certain one among them, that is Brother Philip Long, was touched upon the lips by an angel with a living coal, as was the Prophet Isaiah; a certain one among them, and that was Brother Sylvester, talked with God, as might one friend with another, even as did Moses; a certain one among them did rise by subtlety of intellect even unto the light of divine wisdom, like unto the eagle, which is John the Evangelist, and this was Brother Bernard, the most humble of men, who did expound the Holy Scriptures most learnedly; a certain one among them was sanctified of God, and canonized in Heaven while still living upon this earth, and that was Brother Rufus, a gentleman of Assisi. And thus were all privileged to receive singular signs of sanctity.

Chapter Two

OF BROTHER BERNARD OF QUINTAVALLE, THE FIRST COMPANION OF SAINT FRANCIS.

THE first companion of Saint Francis, Brother Bernard of Assisi, one of the most noble, rich, and wise men of that city, began prudently to consider Saint Francis' exceeding contempt for this world and his great patience amid insults; how that for the space of two long years, being despised of all men, he seemed ever but

the more steadfast in his faith. He spoke to
Saint Francis and said thus: "Brother Francis,
my heart is moved to forsake the world and to
follow after thee in all things that thou shalt
command me." Saint Francis rejoiced in spirit

and spake thus: "Bernard, this of which you
speak is so great and difficult a task that we
must needs take counsel concerning it with Our
Lord Jesus Christ, and pray Him that it may
please Him to show us His sovereign will in the

same, and to teach us how we may execute it."

They set forth and came unto the Bishop's Palace; and there having heard the Mass, and remained absorbed in prayer even unto the third hour of the day, the priest, at the petition of Saint Francis, took up the Missal, and making the sign of the most Holy Cross, did open it three times in the name of Our Lord Jesus Christ; and at the first opening there appeared these words, which Christ spake in the gospel unto the young man who asked of Him the way to be perfect: "If thou wilt be perfect, go and sell that thou hast and give to the poor, and come and follow Me." At the second opening there appeared these words uttered by Christ to the Apostles when He sent them forth to preach: "Provide neither gold, nor silver, nor brass in your purses, nor scrip for your journey, neither two coats, neither shoes, nor yet staves." At the third opening of the Missal there appeared these words: "If any man will come after Me, let him deny himself, and take up his cross, and follow Me." Then said Saint Francis to Bernard, "Go therefore and do that which you have heard; and blessed be Our Lord Jesus Christ, which hath stopped to show us the way of His gospel." Bernard went out and sold all that that he had, — and with great joy did divide all his wealth among widows and orphans, among prisons and monasteries, and among

10

hospitals and pilgrims; and in all things was aided faithfully of Saint Francis.

Bernard likewise received great grace from God, forasmuch as he was often transported in the contemplation of God; and Saint Francis said to him that he was worthy of all reverence, and that he was the true founder of this Order, inasmuch as he was the first who forsook the world, keeping nothing for himself, but giving all to Christ's poor.

Chapter Three

HOW THAT SAINT, BROTHER BERNARD OF ASSISI, WAS DESPATCHED BY SAINT FRANCIS TO BOLOGNA, AND HOW THERE HE TOOK UP HIS ABODE.

INASMUCH as Saint Francis and his companions were called of God and chosen to bear in their hearts and in their lives, and to preach with their tongues, the Cross of Christ they desired to endure shame and opprobrium for the love of Christ rather than to receive worldly honors or the praise of men: thus injuries rejoiced them and honors afflicted them; and thus they passed through the world as Pilgrims and strangers, bearing with them nought save Christ crucified. It happened in the first days of the Order that Saint Francis sent Brother Bernard forth to Bologna, to the end that there he might bear fruit unto God. The children there seeing

11

him in worn and tattered raiment, mocked at him and reviled him as they might have any clown; and Brother Bernard patiently and cheerfully bore all things for the love of Jesus Christ. Soon flocked round about him many boys and men, who pulled him by the cowl, some cast dust upon him and some stones, and Brother Bernard bore all things with meekness. And albeit Patience be a token of Virtue, a learned doctor of laws, seeing so much valor in Brother Bernard, suffering for so many days unmoved by blows said to himself, "Verily, it cannot be but that is a holy man. This is the most high state of religion of which I have heard; and this man and his companions are the most holy men in all the earth, and he who harms the least among them is guilty of a very grievous sin; for every man among them should be held in high honor, inasmuch as he is the true friend of God." And he spake to Brother Bernard, saying, "If you will abide among us, where you may serve God acceptably, I for the salvation of my soul will joyfully give you an abiding-place." Brother Bernard made answer: "Sir, methinks your words are inspired of Our Lord Jesus Christ; and I cheerfully accept this your offer, to the honor and glory of Christ." Then the said Judge with loving kindness led Brother Bernard to his house, and there bestowed upon him the promised lodging and provided for all his costs; and shortly after he himself became a Father, and the especial ally and champion of Brother Bernard. And Brother Bernard, for this his holy conversion, began to be much honored of all men, but he, as a true disciple of Christ, and of the meek and lowly Francis, fearing lest

worldly honors should mar the peace and safety of his soul, departed thence one day and returned to Saint Francis and spake these words: "Father, an abiding-place is found in the city of Bologna: prithee send thither Brothers who may maintain it forasmuch as I no longer profit you

13

aught in that spot; indeed, for the honor which is paid me I fear lest I lose more than I gain." Then Saint Francis, hearing all things in due order, how Our Lord had wrought a great work through Brother Bernard, praised and thanked God, who thus deigned to increase the number of poor followers of the Cross: and then he sent forth his companions into Bologna and into Lombardy, who acquired much land in many places.

Chapter Four

HOW SAINT FRANCIS BLESSED BROTHER BERNARD, AND MADE HIM HIS VICAR WHEN HE CAME TO PASS AWAY FROM THIS LIFE.

SO GREAT was the sanctity of Brother Bernard, that Saint Francis reverenced him much, and many times did praise him, not only in his life, but also in his death. Forasmuch as Saint Francis, being about to die, his mourning sons standing about him devoutly, weeping at the departure of so amiable a father, he asked them: "Where is my firstborn? Come hither to me, my son, that my soul may bless thee before I die." Then Brother Bernard said to Brother Elias, the Vicar of the Order, "Father, go thou to the right hand of the saint, that he may bless thee." Saint Francis, who had lost his sight by reason of his many tears, laid his right hand upon the head of Brother Elias and said, "This is not the head of my firstborn son, Brother Bernard." Then Brother Bernard went and stood by his left hand; and Saint Francis stretching forth his arms in the form of a Cross, laid his right hand upon the head of Brother Bernard and his left hand upon the head of that same Brother Elias, and said to Brother Bernard: "May God the Father and Our Lord Jesus Christ bless thee with every spiritual blessing, and may Christ grant thee all blessings, even as thou art the firstborn, chosen into this Holy Order to give a godly example, to follow Christ in Christian poverty. Thou also hast given thyself as a free-will offering unto God in this Order, a sacrifice pleasing in His sight. Receive, therefore, the blessing of Our Lord Jesus Christ, and of me, His poor servant, blessing everlasting, and all who shall bless thee shall themselves be filled with blessing. Thou art chief among all thy Brethren, and all the Brothers shall bow to thy will." And after the death of Saint Francis the Brethren loved and revered Brother Bernard as a venerable Father; and he, coming to die, many Brothers gathered about him from all quarters of the globe. Brother Bernard, being at the last hour of his death, bade his Brethren lift him up, and spake to them, saying: "My beloved Brethren, you must be mindful that that degree of Religion which I have had you

15

have at this present, and unto that which I now enjoy, you shall yet attain; and I tell you from my soul of souls that I would not for a thousand worlds like unto this have served other Lord than Our Lord Jesus Christ. And for every offence that I have committed I confess myself guilty, and accuse myself before my Savior Jesus and before you. I beseech you, my dearest Brethren, love one another." And after these words his face shone with joy and splendor so exceeding that all the Brothers marveled, and in that rapture his most saintly soul, crowned with glory, passed from this present life into the blessed life of the angels.

Chapter Five

HOW SAINT FRANCIS FASTED FORTY DAYS AND
NIGHTS IN AN ISLAND OF THE LAKE OF PERUGIA,
EATING NO MORE BUT HALF A LOAF.

THAT true servant of Christ, Saint Francis, being in certain things almost another Christ, sent into the world to save the nations, Our Lord and Father God desired to make him in many acts conformable and like unto His Son Jesus Christ; even as we have seen in the venerable college of the twelve companions, and in the admirable Mystery of the Sacred Stigmata, and in the fast lasting throughout the whole term of Lent, which took place after this manner: Saint Francis being once, upon the last day of the carnival, beside the Lake of Perugia in the house of one of his devout followers, he was inspired of God that he should proceed to keep his fast in an island of that lake; wherefore Saint Francis prayed this his follower that he

would bear him over in his boat unto an island of the lake where no man abode; this he should do upon the night of Ash Wednesday, in such manner that they might be seen of none. Saint Francis took nothing with him save two small loaves. And having come to the island, and his friend departing thence, Saint Francis charged him that he should not journey back to fetch him sooner than Maundy-Thursday. And Saint Francis abode there alone, praying and musing upon celestial things. And here he stayed during the whole space of Lent, eating not, neither drinking aught, save the half of one of those small loaves, according as his faithful follower found him when he crossed over to him on Maundy-Thursday. It is believed that Saint Francis did partake out of reverence for the fasting of the blessed Christ, Who fasted forty days and forty nights, partaking of no bodily food; and thus with that half loaf he drove far from him the venom of Vainglory, and following after Christ fasted forty days and forty nights. And then in that place where Francis did such marvelous feats of abstinence God the Lord wrought many miracles through his merits: for the which thing men began to build houses and to dwell there; and in a brief space a castle stood therein, and this was the home of the Brethren, and it was called by the name of the island; and even unto this present time the men and the women of that castle display great reverence and devotion upon that spot where Saint Francis fasted as has been here set forth.

Chapter Six

SAINT FRANCIS sojourned upon a time in the Convent of Portiuncula with Brother Maximus of Marignano, a man of much sanctity, discretion, and grace in discoursing of God. One day Brother Maximus, desiring to know whether the humility of the saint were unfeigned, mockingly cried out to him, "Wherefore followeth the whole world after thee, and why doth every man desire to see and to hear and to obey thee? Thou art not fair to see, thou hast no great learning, neither art thou noble." Hearing this, Saint Francis lifted his face to Heaven, then knelt and gave praise and glory to God, after which he turned to Brother Maximus and said, "Would you know wherefore men follow after me? This grace I have from the eyes of the Most High God, which in all places behold the godly and the ungodly: forasmuch as those most holy eyes never yet beheld a greater sinner, nor yet to do that marvelous work which He willeth to accomplish has He found a viler creature upon earth. And therefore hath He chosen me, to confound the Nobility and the Grandeur and the Strength and the

19

Beauty and the Wisdom of the world, that it may be made known that all Virtue and all Goodness are from Him and not from His creatures, and that none may glory in his own sight; but that all who glory may glory in the Lord, unto whom be all glory and honor for ever and ever Amen." Then Brother Maximus at so humble an answer, uttered with such fervor, knew of a surety that the humility of Saint Francis was unfeigned.

Chapter Seven

HOW SAINT CLARA ATE WITH SAINT FRANCIS AND WITH HIS BROTHER MONKS IN ST. MARY OF THE ANGELS.

S AINT FRANCIS, when he was at Assisi, oft-times visited Saint Clara, giving her holy teachings; and she having the greatest desire to eat with him but once, and entreating him many times to this end, he would never grant her that consolation. Hence his companions said to Saint Francis: "Father, to us it seems that such severity is not in accordance with Divine Charity, that Sister Clara, a virgin so saintly, should not find favor in your sight to gain so small a thing as to eat with you; and especially considering that she through your preaching forsook riches and all the pomps of this world; and verily, were she to ask you a much greater grace

20

than this, you should grant it to your spiritual child." Then Saint Francis said: "Since it seems meet to you, it seems so also unto me. But that she may be the more consoled, I desire that this meal should be eaten in the Church of St. Mary of the Angels, forasmuch as she has long been cloistered in St. Damian: therefore it will rejoice her much to see the Church of St. Mary, where her locks were shorn off and she was made the bride of Jesus Christ; and there we will eat together in the name of God." When the day came appointed for this, Saint Clara left her Convent with one companion, accompanied by the companions of Saint Francis, and came to St. Mary of the Angels. And Saint Francis ordered the cloth to be laid in their midst upon the bare ground, as he was wont to do. And Saint Francis and Saint Clara sat down together, and one of the comrades of Saint Francis with Saint Clara's companion, and then all their other companions took their places humbly. And for the first dish Saint Francis began to talk of God so nobly, so wondrous well, that the abundance of the Divine grace descending upon them, they were all transported as it were to Heaven. And with eyes and hands raised to Heaven, the men of Assisi and of Bettona, and of the country round about, saw how St. Mary of the Angels, and all that place, and the wood which stood beside it, burned fiercely; where-

21

for the people of Assisi in great haste ran thither to put out the fire, truly thinking that everything was burning. But on reaching the spot, and finding no flames, they entered in, and found Saint Francis with Saint Clara, and with all their companions, absorbed in the contemplation of God, and sitting around that humble board. Whence they perceived that those were divine flames, which God had caused to appear miraculously, to signify the Fire of the Divine Love with which the souls of those holy monks and nuns were consumed. Then after a great space Saint Francis returning to himself, and likewise Saint Clara, together with the others, and feeling themselves much comforted by the spiritual food, they cared little for bodily sustenance. And thus, this blessed meal was ended.

Chapter Eight

HOW SAINT FRANCIS RECEIVED THE ADVICE OF SAINT CLARA AND OF HOLY BROTHER SYLVESTER, THAT HE SHOULD GO FORTH AND PREACH; AND HE CREATED THE THIRD ORDER, AND PREACHED TO THE BIRDS AND SILENCED THE YOUNG SWALLOWS.

SAINT FRANCIS, shortly after his conversion, having already gathered together many companions and received them into the Order, fell into deep thought and into grave doubt as to what he should do, — whether he should devote himself wholly to prayer, or whether he should sometimes preach; and on this subject he greatly desired to know the will of God. He called Brother Maximus, and spake to him thus: "Go to Sister Clara and tell her from me that she, with certain of her most spiritual companions, shall pray devoutly to God that it may please Him to reveal to me whether it is better that I should devote myself to preaching, or merely to prayer. And then go to Brother Sylvester and say the same words." Brother Maximus returned to Saint Francis who after some time received him with the utmost affection. "What does my Lord and Master Jesus Christ command me to do?" Brother Maximus made answer: "Both to Brother Sylvester and to Sister Clara, with her Sisters, Christ has made manifest that it is His will that you shall go forth into the world to preach; forasmuch as He did not call you for yourself alone, but even also for the salvation of others." And then Saint Francis rose up with the greatest fervor, saying, "Let us go forth in the name of God." And he took for his companions Brother Maximus and Brother Andrew; and going forth filled with the things of the spirit they came to a castle, which is called Savurniano, and Saint Francis began to preach; and he first commanded the swallows to keep silence so long as until he

should have preached; and the swallows obeyed
him; and he preached in this place with such
fervor that all the men and the women in that
castle, from devotion, would have followed
after him. And then he created the Third Order, for the universal salvation of all men; and

thus leaving many consoled and well disposed
to penitence, he departed from thence and
came to Cannajo and Bevagno. And passing
on his way with the selfsame fervor, he raised
his eyes and saw certain trees by the roadside
in which were an infinite multitude of birds; at

which Saint Francis marveled greatly, and said to his companions, "Await me here in the road, and I will go and preach to my Sisters the birds."

Finally, his preaching ended, Saint Francis made them the sign of the Cross and gave them leave to depart; and then all those birds rose into the air with wondrous songs; and then, according to the Cross which Saint Francis had made them, they divided into four parts; and each band went away singing marvelous songs; signifying by this how that Saint Francis, the Ensign of the Cross of Christ, had come to preach to them; and had made the sign of the Cross over them, according to which they had scattered to the four quarters of the globe. Thus the preaching of the Cross of Christ renewed by Saint Francis was by him and his brethren borne throughout the whole world; which brethren, even as the birds, possessed nothing of this world's goods, but committed their life to the sole and only providence of God.

Chapter Nine

OF A VERY FAIR VISION, SEEN BY A YOUNG FRIAR, WHO HELD THE COWL IN SUCH ABOMINATION THAT HE WAS DISPOSED TO LAY ASIDE HIS HABIT AND FORSAKE THE ORDER.

A CERTAIN very noble and delicate youth entered the Order of Saint Francis; the which after the space of some days, by the instigation

of the devil, began to hold the Habit which he
wore in abomination, and its length and harsh-
ness seemed to him an unbearable burden. And
his distaste for the Religious Life ever increas-
ing, he at last proposed to give up the Habit and
return to the world. It had become his custom,
according as he had been taught, to kneel most
reverently at whatsoever hour he might pass
before the altar of the Convent whereon the
Body of Christ was kept, and drawing his cowl
over his head, to bow low with crossed arms. It
happened, that upon the self-same night wherein he was to depart from the Order, he was
forced to pass before the Convent Altar; and
as was his wont, he knelt and made a humble
reverence. And suddenly he was rapt in an
ecstasy, and was shown by God a wondrous
vision, forasmuch as he saw before him an almost infinite number of saints, walking as in
procession, two by two, arrayed in most pre-
cious robes of linen, and their faces and their
hands shone like the sun, and they passed along
with angelic sounds; among which saints were
two more nobly clad than all the others, and
they were set round about with such lustre that
all who gazed upon them were filled with exceeding great awe; and almost at the end of
the procession he saw one decked with such
glory that he seemed a new-made knight, more
honored than the rest. This youth beholding the

26

vision, marveled and knew not what this procession meant, and he ventured not to ask, but remained struck dumb with the delight of it. And nevertheless all the procession having passed him by, he plucked up his spirits and ran forthwith to the last men in it; and asked: "Oh, my Beloved, I pray that you tell me who are these wondrous beings?" And they answered: "Know, O son, that we are all Gray Friars, who come hither from the splendors of Paradise." And he again questioned them, saying: "Who are yonder two, who shine yet more radiant than the rest?" They made answer: "Those are Saint Francis and Saint Antony; and that last, so greatly honored, is a Holy Brother who died but newly; who, forasmuch as he fought valiantly against all temptation, and persevered unto the end, we conduct in triumph to the glories of Paradise; and these garments of fair linen are given us of God in exchange for the coarse tunics which patiently we wore in the religious order; and the glorious lustre which you see round about us is given us of God for the humility and patience and for the holy poverty and obedience and chastity which we observed unto the end. And therefore, son, hold it not hard to bear the sackcloth of religion which is so fruitful of reward; forasmuch, as if with the sackcloth of Saint Francis, for love of Christ, you despise the world, and mortify the

27

flesh, and fight a good fight against the foul fiend, you shall have raiment like unto that which we do wear, and a glory of light." And having heard these words, the youth returned to his senses, and greatly comforted, he drove far from him all temptation, and confessed his sin before his Superior and the Brethren; and from that time forth he ardently longed for asperity of penitence and of attire, and ended his life in the Order in great holiness.

Chapter Ten

HOW THE GRAPES IN THE VINEYARD OF THE PRIEST OF RIETI, IN WHOSE HOUSE SAINT FRANCIS PRAYED, WERE TRAMPLED AND PLUCKED BY THE MANY PEOPLE WHICH CAME THITHER TO HIM; AND THEN MIRACULOUSLY MADE MORE WINE THAN EVER BEFORE, EVEN AS SAINT FRANCIS HAD PROMISED.

SAINT FRANCIS being once afflicted with a grievous malady of the eyes, Cardinal Ugolino, Protector of the Order, for the great love he bore him, wrote bidding him come to Rieti, where were most excellent doctors for the eyes. Saint Francis called his companion, with exceeding great joy, and said, "Let us set forth to the Cardinal." He took his way towards Rieti, and when he had drawn near, so vast a multitude of people came forth to meet him, that he could not therefore enter into the city; but he went to a church, which was distant perhaps two miles from the town. The citizens ran thither in such numbers to behold him, that the vineyard of the said church was laid waste, and the grapes were all gathered; at which the Priest

was greatly grieved within himself, and repented that he had received Saint Francis. The Priest's thought being revealed of God to Saint Francis, he called him before him, saying: "Beloved Father, how many measures of wine does your vineyard yield you in the best of years?" He answered, "Twelve measures." Saint Francis said: "I pray you, Father, patiently to permit me to abide with you yet a few days and suffer every man to pluck the grapes of this your vineyard, for the love of God, and of me a poor beggar; and I promise you in the name of my Master Christ Jesus, that it shall yield you every year twenty measures." And this did Saint Francis to the end that he might sojourn there, where he reaped a rich harvest of souls, from the multitude that came thither; many of whom departed thence drunk with Divine Love, and forsook the world. The Priest had faith in the promise of Saint Francis, and freely suffered all who came to pluck the grapes. Wonderful to relate! The time for the vintage came, and the Priest gathered in the scanty clusters, and placed them in the press and trod them out, and according to the promise of Saint Francis they yielded him twenty measures of the best wine. By which miracle is manifestly set forth, that as by the merits of Saint Francis the vine stripped of its grapes yet abounded in wine, so the Christian people, made bare of virtues by their sins, through the merits and doctrine of Saint Francis ofttimes abound in the good fruits of repentance.

Chapter Eleven

OF THE MOST HOLY MIRACLE, WHICH SAINT
FRANCIS PERFORMED, WHEN HE CONVERTED
THE VERY FIERCE WOLF AT GUBBIO.

IN THE days when Saint Francis dwelt in the
city of Gubbio, there appeared in that region
a very great, terrible, and fierce Wolf, the which
not only devoured animals, but even also men.
Then Saint Francis, having compassion upon
the men of that land, desired to go forth unto
this Wolf, and drawing near to him, Saint
Francis made the sign of the Most Holy Cross,
and called unto him: "Come hither, Brother
Wolf; I command you in the name of Christ
Jesus, that you do no manner of evil either
to me or to any other man." Wonderful to
relate! Immediately that Saint Francis made
the sign of the Cross, the terrible Wolf closed
his jaws and gave over running; and came meekly as any lamb, and laid himself down at the
feet of Saint Francis. And thereupon Saint Francis said: "Brother Wolf, you have done great
evil, killing and devouring God's creatures without His sovereign leave. And not only have you
killed and devoured beasts, but you have dared
to kill men, made in the image of God; and
all the people cry out. But I desire, Brother
Wolf, to make peace between you and them, so
that you offend no more; inasmuch as it pleases

you to keep this peace, I promise you that I
will see to it that your living shall be given
you continually, so long as you shall live, by the
men of this country forasmuch as I am well
aware that hunger has caused you every crime.
But since I get for you this grace, I require,
Brother Wolf, your promise never again to do
harm to any human being, neither to any beast.
I desire you to give me some token of this your
promise, although I have full faith in your loy-
alty." And Saint Francis stretching forth his
hand, the Wolf lifted up his right paw and con-
fidingly laid it in the hand of Saint Francis. And
then Saint Francis said: "Brother Wolf, I charge
you in the name of Christ Jesus that you now
follow me, and we will go forth and conclude
this peace in God's name." And the Wolf obe-
diently followed after him, like any lamb; so
that the citizens, seeing this, marveled greatly.
Then Saint Francis rose up and began to preach
to them: "Inasmuch as for your sins, God hath
permitted certain evil things and far more dan-
gerous as are the flames of hell, which endure
eternally for the damned, than is the wrath of
the Wolf, which can but kill the body, — so
much more therefore should ye fear the jaws of
hell, when the mouth of one small animal can
terrify and alarm so vast a multitude! Turn then,
my Beloved, unto God, and repent worthily of
your sins." And having preached, Saint Francis

32

said: "Hearken, my Brethren: "Brother Wolf
hath promised to make peace with you and you
must promise henceforth to give him daily all
that is needful to him." Then all the people with
one accord promised to feed him continually.
And Saint Francis said: "Brother Wolf, I desire

that even as you gave me your promise outside
the gates, so here before all these people you
shall give me a token of your good faith." Then
the Wolf, lifting up his right paw, laid it in the
hand of Saint Francis. Upon this action and

upon those which had gone before, there was such marveling in all the people, both at the devotion of the Saint, and at the novelty of the miracle, and at the peace with the Wolf, that all began to cry aloud unto Heaven, praising and blessing God, that had sent unto them Saint Francis.

Chapter Twelve

HOW SAINT FRANCIS ON A TIME TAMED THE WILD TURTLE-DOVES.

A BOY one day took a number of turtle-doves, and carrying them to the market-place for sale, he met Saint Francis, who ever felt singular compassion for all gentle animals. Gazing at these turtle-doves with pitiful eyes, he said to the boy: "Oh, good youth, give them to me, I pray you; nor suffer birds so meek and gentle, to whom chaste, humble, and faithful souls are likened in the Scriptures, to fall into the hands of cruel men, who will slay them." The boy, suddenly inspired of God, gave them all to Saint Francis; and he receiving them began to speak sweetly unto them: "O my Sisters, chaste and innocent doves, why did ye suffer yourselves to be taken? I would now rescue you from death, and make nests for you, that ye may increase and bring forth young, according to the command of the Lord our God." And Saint Francis went forth, and made nests for every one; and they, using them, began to lay eggs, and to bring forth young before the Friars; and so tame were they and consorted so freely with Saint Francis and the other Friars, as they had been hens and ever fed from their hands, and departed not from among them, until Saint Francis with his blessing gave them leave to fly thence. And to the boy who gave them to him Saint Francis said: "Son, you shall yet be a Brother in this Order, and shall serve Christ Jesus worthily," and so it was; forasmuch as the boy became a Friar and lived in the Order with great sanctity.

Chapter Thirteen

HOW SAINT FRANCIS MIRACULOUSLY HEALED THE LEPER IN BODY AND SOUL.

THAT true disciple of Christ, Saint Francis strove ever to follow Christ, the Perfect Way, whence it ofttimes befell by divine action that whereas he healed a man's body, God did heal his soul in that selfsame hour, even as we read of Christ. And inasmuch as he not only freely became the servant of lepers, but furthermore ordered that the Brothers of his Order, journeying anywhere in this world, should become the servants of lepers for the love of Christ, it fell out that at a Convent near which Saint Francis was then abiding, the Brethren

35

were serving in a hospital for lepers and infirm; in which was a leper so intolerable and so arrogant that all men deemed that he was possessed of a devil, forasmuch as alike with words and blows he terribly reviled all them that served him; nay, yet worse, he scandalously blasphemed against the blessed Christ and his most Holy Mother the Virgin Mary, so that none could be found who could or would serve him. And albeit the Brethren truly study meekly to endure injuries and insults to themselves, to the end that patience may have her perfect work, nevertheless, those to Christ and his Mother their consciences could not suffer, and every man among them determined to leave the said leper: but this they would not do before they had duly declared their purpose unto Saint Francis. Then came Saint Francis unto that perverse leper saying: "God grant thee peace, my beloved Brother." The leper made answer, "What peace can I have of God, Which hath robbed me of every good thing, and hath made me all corrupt and stinking. Can I endure the pain that torments me night and day? And far worse do I suffer from the brethren whom you have given me to wait upon me, and they serve me not as they should." Then Saint Francis knowing by a revelation that this leper was possessed of an evil spirit entreated God piously for him. "My Son, I myself will serve you, since

36

you are ill-content with the others." "It pleaseth me well," said the sick man; "but what can you do for me more than the others?" Saint Francis answered, "Whatsoever you would that I should do." Said the leper, "I would that you wash me, every inch of me; forasmuch as so terribly

I stink that I myself can ill endure it." Then Saint Francis straight commanded water to be heated with many sweet-smelling herbs; then stripping him, he began to wash him with his own hands, and by a divine miracle, whereso-

ever Saint Francis laid his holy hands upon him
the leprosy left him. And even as his flesh began to heal, so too his soul began to be made
whole! Hence the leper seeing himself begin-
ning to be cured, began to have great repentance
for his sins, and began to weep bitterly; for as
his body was cleansed of the leprosy from
without by the washing of the water, even so
his soul was cleansed of sin from within by
correction and tears. And being wholly healed,
alike in body and in soul, he humbly confessed
himself guilty, and cried aloud, weeping: "Woe
unto me, for I am worthy of hell-fire for the
insults which I have heaped upon the Brethren,
and for the blasphemy which I have manifested
towards God." Hence for two long weeks he
persevered in bitter tears for his sins, and in be-
seeching mercy from God, making ample con-
fession to the Priest. And Saint Francis, seeing
so plain a miracle, which God had wrought by
his hand, gave thanks to the Lord and departed
thence, going into remote countries: forasmuch
as from Humility he desired to flee all Vainglory, and in all his acts sought only the Glory
of God and not his own.

Chapter Fourteen

THE great favor which our Lord ofttimes showed to those who forseek the world for love of Christ is set forth in Brother Bernard of Quintavelle, who, after taking on the Habit of Saint Francis, was very many times absorbed in God, in the contemplation of celestial things. It happened upon a time that being in church hearkening to the Mass, and standing with his whole mind bent on God, he became so absorbed that at the Elevation of the Host he was conscious of naught, neither knelt, nor bared his head; but without once winking, did stand steadfastly gazing from the hour of Matins until Nones, as if insensible: and after Nones, returning to himself, did go about the Convent crying in tones of awe and wonder: "O Brothers! There is no man in this land so great, or so noble, to whom, were he promised a most beauteous palace filled with gold, it were not easy to bear most loathsome burdens, to gain so rare a treasure." Now the mind of the aforesaid Brother Bernard was so bent upon this Celestial Treasure promised to all true lovers of God, that for fifteen years continually he went ever with his face upraised to Heaven; and in all that time he satisfied never his hunger at table, albeit he ate of that which was put before him a little, forasmuch as he said that the mere fact of eating naught constitutes not perfect abstinence, but true abstinence is to be temperate

in all things which are savory in the mouth; and thereby he attained to such clearness of intellect that even the great doctors of the church had recourse to him for the solution of knotty questions and hard passages of Scripture; and he made plain every puzzle to them, and inasmuch as his mind was freed and abstracted from all earthly things, he, after the manner of a swallow, flew oft aloft in thought; hence sometimes thirty days he would abide alone upon the top of very high mountains musing upon celestial matters. For this excellent grace, given him of God, Saint Francis gladly and often held converse with him both night and day. Hence they were at certain times found the whole night long absorbed in God in the thick wood, where they had met together to discourse of Him.

Chapter Fifteen

OF THE GLORIOUS SERMON WHICH SAINT FRANCIS AND BROTHER RUFUS PREACHED AT ASSISI.

Brother Rufus, through continual contemplation, grew to be so absorbed in God that he became almost dumb and insensible, and but very rarely spoke; and withal he had not the grace nor the eloquence to preach: and nevertheless Saint Francis charged him that he should go to Assisi, and should preach to the people even as the Lord should inspire him. To which Brother Rufus made answer: "Reverend Father, I beseech you, send me not forth, as you are well aware that I have no grace in preaching, and am simple and unlearned." And then said Saint Francis: "Forasmuch as you have not

obeyed promptly, I command you by your
sacred vow of Obedience that you go, clad
only in your breeches, unto Assisi, and enter
there a church and preach to the people." Upon this command the said Brother Rufus laid
off his raiment and went to Assisi and entered
into a church, went up into the pulpit and began
to preach; at which thing the men and boys began to laugh, and said, "Lo, one who doth penitence, lest he grow proud and vain." Meantime
Saint Francis, pondering on the ready obedience
of Brother Rufus, which was one of the noblest
gentlemen of Assisi, and of the hard command
which he had laid upon him, began to reproach
himself, saying, "Whence hast thou such presumption that thou shouldst command Brother
Rufus to go forth and preach to the people even
as he were mad? In God's name, go forth thou
likewise, and prove for thyself even that thou
hast commanded of others." And in the ardor
of his spirit, he also laid off his raiment and went
forth to Assisi, and with him went Brother Leo
bearing his Habit and that of Brother Rufus.
And the men of Assisi seeing them in like plight,
scoffed at them, holding that they with Brother
Rufus were made mad by much Penitence. Saint
Francis entered into the church where Brother
Rufus was preaching, and went up into the
pulpit; and he began to preach so marvelously
of the Vanity of the world, of holy Penitence,

of voluntary Poverty, and of the longing after the Celestial Kingdom, and of the nakedness and scorn of the Passion of our Lord Jesus Christ, that all they who heard his preaching began to weep violently with admirable devotion and contrition; and not only here, but throughout all Assisi, upon that day such floods of tears were shed for Christ's Passion, that nothing similar was ever seen. And the people being thus consoled by the act of Saint Francis and Brother Rufus, Saint Francis clad again both Brother Rufus and himself; and they returned back to the Convent of Portiuncula, praising and glorifying God, Who had given them grace to win the victory over self by their self-contempt, and to edify the flock of Christ Jesus by their good example, and to show what it is to despise the world; and that day so great was the devotion which the people felt for them, that he held himself blessed who could but touch the hem of their garments.

Chapter Sixteen

HOW SAINT FRANCIS KNEW THE SECRET SOULS OF HIS BRETHREN.

EVEN as our Lord Jesus Christ saith in the gospel, "I know my sheep and they know me," etc., so the blessed Father Saint Francis knew all the merits of his companions by divine revelations, and even so was made aware of their defects; for the which thing he knew how to provide for each the best remedy, which is to say, he humbled the Proud, exalted the Lowly, inveighed against Vice, and lauded Virtue. Among the same we learn that Saint Francis once being with his companions discoursing of God, Brother Rufus was not among them, but was lost in a muse in the midst of the woods; proceeding with their discourse of God, lo! Brother Rufus came forth from the wood and passed by somewhat remote from them. Then Saint Francis seeing him, turned again to his companions and asked them, saying: "Tell me, whose think you is the holiest soul which God hath sent into the world?" And they answered that they believed it to be his own. And Saint Francis said: "Beloved Brethren, I know myself to be the most unworthy and the vilest of men; but see ye not that same Brother Rufus, who even now came forth from the wood? God hath revealed to me that his soul is one of the three most holy souls in the world: and verily I say that I should not hesitate to call him Saint Rufus while he yet lives, forasmuch as his soul is confirmed in grace and sanctified and canonized in Heaven of our Lord Jesus Christ." How Saint Francis likewise knew the faults of his Brethren may be clearly seen in Brother Elias, whom he reproved for his pride; and in Brother

John of the Choir, to whom he did prophesy that he should go out and hang himself by the neck; and in that Friar whom the devil held fast by the throat when he was corrected for his disobedience; and in many other Friars, whose secret faults and virtues he knew clearly through a revelation from Christ.

Chapter Seventeen

HOW BROTHER MAXIMUS ENTREATED OF CHRIST THE VIRTUE OF MEEKNESS.

THE first companions of Saint Francis strove with all their strength to be poor in worldly goods and rich in virtues, by which they might gain true riches, celestial and eternal. One day, that they being met together to talk of God, one of them related this parable: "There was a certain man who had great gifts alike for a life of action and of contemplation, and withal had such exceeding meekness, that he held himself as the greatest of sinners: which meekness strengthened him in grace, and made him grow continually in virtue and in the favor of God." Brother Maximus hearing such marvelous things concerning meekness began to be so inflamed with longing for this virtue that, raising his eyes with great fervor to Heaven, he made a vow never more to be merry until he should feel the said virtue abiding perfectly within him; and from that time forth he would pass almost the entire day shut up within his cell, mortifying himself with fasts, vigils and prayers, to the end that he might wring from Him this virtue, wanting which he held himself worthy of hell. And a Voice came down from Heaven, and it said: "What will you give to have this grace that you ask?" Brother Maximus replied: "Lord, I will give the eyes out of my head." And Christ said to him: "And I desire that you have the grace, and likewise the eyes." And saying this, the Voice vanished; and Brother Maximus was left behind filled with so much grace of the desired virtue of meekness and of the Light of God, that from that time forth he went ever rejoicing; and ofttimes when he prayed, did rejoice aloud, making a dull noise like that of a dove, — "*oo, oo, oo,*" — and with a shining countenance and a light heart he would linger thus lost in contemplation; and withal, being become very meek, he held himself to be less than all other men.

Chapter Eighteen

HOW SAINT LOUIS, KING OF FRANCE, WENT IN PERSON, IN THE GUISE OF A PILGRIM, TO PERUGIA, TO VISIT HOLY BROTHER GUY.

SAINT LOUIS, King of France, once went on a pilgrimage to see the holy places of the world: and hearing the exceeding great fame of the sanctity of Brother Guy, who was one of the first followers of Saint Francis, he determined to visit him in person in Perugia. And drawing nigh to the gate of the Monastery, in the guise of a poor and unknown pilgrim, with but a few companions, he most persistently demanded Brother Guy. The gate-keeper then went to Brother Guy and told him that a pilgrim stood without the gate and asked for him: and God revealed and made known to him that this was the King of France: at which suddenly he with great fervor left his cell and ran forth to the gate; and without further questioning, and before even they had set eyes each upon the other, kneeling with extreme devotion, they embraced, but withal they spoke no word. And having remained thus for a space without speaking a word together, Saint Louis departed thence on his journey, and Brother Guy returned again to his cell. The King being departed, a Friar asked one among his Brethren who that man might be who had so ardently embraced Brother Guy; and he made answer that it was Louis, King of France. The Monks were sore afflicted that Brother Guy had spoken no word with him; and reproving him said: "O Brother Guy, wherefore were you so churlish, as when so holy a King came hither from France to hear wise words from your lips, you spake not unto him?" Brother Guy made answer: "My beloved Brothers, marvel not hereat: forasmuch as neither I could speak a word to him nor he to me; inasmuch as soon as we were embraced, the light of Divine Wisdom revealed and laid bare his heart to me and mine to him; and thus by Divine Authority gazing each into the other's heart, we knew far better those things which he might have spoken to me and I to him, than had we spoken them with our lips, and with greater comfort than had we striven to set forth with our voice those things which we felt in our hearts; whereas the human tongue being but faulty and ill-fitted to express clearly the secret mysteries of God, it would have rather added to our discomfiture than our consolation; wherefore know that the King departed hence from me wondrous well content and comforted in spirit."

Chapter Nineteen

HOW SAINT FRANCIS SET FORTH THE FAIR VISION
WHICH BROTHER LEO SAW.

UPON a time Saint Francis was sore infirm, and Brother Leo served him; and Brother Leo, being at prayer beside Saint Francis, was rapt in ecstasy, and borne in spirit to an exceeding great stream, broad and brawling. And standing there to note who should pass over, he saw certain heavily-laden Friars enter the flood, the which were straightway beaten down by the rushing waters and were drowned; certain others came almost over to the other shore; who all, from the violence of the flood and from the burdens which they bare upon their backs, fell at last and perished miserably. Seeing this, Brother Leo was much moved to pity: and suddenly standing thus, behold there came a great multitude of Monks, without burden or weight or any other thing, whose countenances shone with the light of Holy Poverty; and they entered upon the waters, and passed over without any danger; and seeing this, Brother Leo returned to himself. And then Saint Francis, feeling in spirit that Brother Leo had seen some vision, called him unto his bedside and asked him concerning those things which he had seen. And Brother Leo relating duly all his vision, Saint Francis said: "That which you have seen is true. The great river is this world; the Brethren which were drowned in the flood are they who forsake the calling of the Evangelists; but they who passed over unharmed are those Monks who seek after naught earthly or carnal, neither possess aught of this world's goods, but are well content, following Christ naked on the Cross; and they do bear cheerfully and willingly the burden and the sweet yoke of Christ and of the sacred vow of Obedience; and hence they pass easily from temporal unto Eternal Life."

Chapter Twenty

OF THE MIRACLE WHICH GOD PERFORMED WHEN
SAINT ANTONY, BEING AT RIMINI, PREACHED TO
THE FISHES OF THE SEA.

OUR Blessed Lord, desiring to set forth the
great sanctity of His faithful servant Saint
Antony, how devout a thing it was to hear his
preaching and his Holy Doctrines, He reproved
the folly of heretics and infidels through un-
reasoning beasts, notably the fishes, as of old
in the Bible He chid the ignorance of Balaam
through the mouth of the Ass. Hence, Saint Antony being at Rimini, where there was a great
multitude of heretics, desiring to bring them
back to the light of the true faith, for many days
did preach to them the faith of Christ and of the
Holy Scriptures: but they, not only consenting
not to his Holy Words, but refusing to hearken
unto him, Saint Antony one day by Divine In-
spiration went forth to the banks of the river,
close beside the sea; and standing thus betwixt
sea and stream, he began to speak in the guise
of a sermon in the Name of God unto the fishes:
"Hear the Word of God, ye fishes, since heretics and infidels are loath to listen to it"; and
suddenly there came towards him so great a
multitude of fishes as had never been seen in
that sea, or in that stream; and all held their
heads up out of the water, and all turned atten-

tively towards the face of Saint Antony, and the greatest peace and order prevailed: insomuch that next the shore stood the lesser fish, and after them came the middle fish, and still after them, where the water was deepest, stood the larger fish. The fish being thus ranged in order, Saint Antony began solemnly to preach: "My Brothers the fish, you are greatly bounden, so far as in you lies, to thank your Creator that He hath given you so noble an element for your habitation; so that at your pleasure you have fresh waters and salt; and He hath given you many shelters against storm. He hath also given you food, by which you may live. To you was it granted, by God's command, to preserve the prophet Jonah, and after the third day to cast him up upon the land safe and sound. You were the food of the everlasting King Christ Jesus; before the resurrection and after it, by a strange mystery; for the which things greatly are you bounden to raise and bless God." Upon these words of Saint Antony the fishes began to ope their mouths, and to bow their heads; and by these and other signs of reverence, according as it was possible to them, they praised God. Then Saint Antony seeing such reverence in the fishes towards God their Creator, rejoicing in spirit, cried aloud: "Blessed be the eternal God, since fishes of the waters honor Him far more than heretic men." And as

Saint Antony continued his preaching, the multitude of fishes was increased yet more. Upon this miracle the people of the town began to hasten forth, and among them were also the aforesaid heretics; the which, seeing so manifest

a miracle, felt their hearts sorely pricked, and fell with one accord at Saint Antony's feet. Then Saint Antony began to preach of the Catholic faith; and so nobly did he discourse, that he converted all those heretics and turned them to the true faith of Christ; and all the faithful with great joy were confirmed in their faith.

Chapter Twenty-one

OF THE MARVELOUS SERMON WHICH WAS
PREACHED IN THE CONSISTORY BY SAINT AN-
TONY OF PADUA, A GRAY FRIAR.

SAINT ANTONY of Padua, one of the chosen
Disciples and companions of Saint Francis,
who was called of Saint Francis his Vicar, once
preached in the Consistory before the Pope and
his Cardinals; in which Consistory there were
men of divers nations; namely, Greeks, Latins,
French, Germans, Slavs, and English, and men
speaking other divers tongues. Fired by the
Holy Ghost, so efficaciously, so devoutly, so
sweetly, and so clearly did he set forth the
Word of God, that all they which were present
at the Consistory, of whatsoever divers tongues
they were, clearly understood all his words dis-
tinctly, even as he had spoken in the language
of each man among them; and they all were
struck dumb with amaze, and it seemed as that
ancient miracle of the Apostles had been renewed, when as at the time of the Pentecost
they spake by virtue of the Holy Ghost in every
tongue; and they said one to another with ad-
miration and awe: "Is not he who preaches
come out from Spain? and how do we hear in
his discourse every man of us the speech of
his own land?" Likewise the Pope, considering

and marveling at the profundity of his words, said: "Verily this man is the Ark of the Covenant and the Vehicle of the Holy Gospel."

Chapter Twenty-two

HOW, BEING INFIRM, SAINT CLARA WAS BORNE BY A MIRACLE UNTO THE CHURCH OF SAINT FRANCIS, UPON CHRISTMAS NIGHT.

SAINT CLARA being once infirm of body could not go forth to say Mass with the other Nuns, at the solemn feast of the Nativity of Christ but remained behind in bed ill content that she could not receive that spiritual comfort. But Jesus Christ, her Heavenly Spouse, loath to leave her so, had her borne by miraculous power unto the Church of St. Francis, and thus was she present at the office of Matins and at the Midnight Mass; moreover, did receive Holy Communion, and was then transported again to her bed. The Nuns returning from the service at St. Damian's, said to her: "Oh, our Mother, what exceeding consolation has been ours at this sacred feast of the Nativity! Would it had pleased God that you might have been among us!" And Saint Clara replied: "Thanksgiving give I unto Our Lord Christ Jesus; for I have witnessed every rite of this most holy night. By the grace of our Lord Jesus Christ,

I was present in the church of my venerable
Father Saint Francis, and heard all the Office
with my bodily as well as my spiritual ears, and
the sound of the organ as it was played; and
there too I did partake of the most Holy Communion and now do rejoice most greatly and
thank our Lord Jesus Christ."

Chapter Twenty-three

HOW SAINT CLARA, AT THE COMMAND OF THE
POPE, BLESSED THE BREAD WHICH WAS ON THE
TABLE: WHEREAT ON EVERY LOAF WAS SEEN
THE SIGN OF THE HOLY CROSS.

SAINT CLARA, the most devout follower of the
Cross of Christ, and the noble offspring of
Saint Francis, was of such sanctity that not
alone Bishops and Cardinals but even the Pope
himself longed with great affection to see and to
hear her, and many times visited her in person.
The Holy Father once went to Monistero to
hear her converse of celestial and divine things;
and being thus met together, Saint Clara meantime bade them make ready the tables, and place
upon them bread, to the end that the Holy
Father might bless it; whence, her spiritual discourse completed, Saint Clara, kneeling with
great reverence, prayed him that it might please
him to bless the bread upon the table. The Holy

Father replied: "Sister Clara, most faithful among women, I desire that you do bless these loaves, making above them the sign of Christ's Holy Cross, to which you have given yourself entirely, body and soul." Saint Clara said: "Pardon me, Most Holy Father, for I should be

worthy of great reproach if before the face of Christ's Vicar on earth, I, who am but a vile and silly woman, should venture to give such blessing." And the Pope made answer: "To the end that it be not reputed presumption, but merely righteous submission, I charge you, by your sacred vow of Obedience, to make the sign of the most Holy Cross above these loaves, blessing them in the name of God." Then Saint Clara did devoutly bless the bread with the sign of the most Holy Cross. Wonderful to relate! Suddenly upon all those loaves appeared the sign of the Cross most beauteously carven. Then of those loaves a part was eaten, and a part preserved in token of the miracle. And the Holy Father, after that he had seen that miracle, partaking of the said bread and giving thanks to God, departed thence, leaving Saint Clara with his blessing.

Chapter Twenty-four

OF THE VISION OF BROTHER JOHN OF VERNIA, WHEREIN HE KNEW THE WHOLE ORDER OF THE HOLY TRINITY.

THE aforesaid Brother John of Vernia, forasmuch as he had perfectly abjured every temporal comfort and delight, and had put all his pleasure and all his hope in God, Divine Bounty gave him wondrous revelations, especially at the high feasts of Christ; whence the solemn feast of Christ's Nativity once drawing nigh, whereon he surely awaited comfort from God, the Holy Ghost poured into his soul such great love and longing for the brotherly affection of Christ, through the which He did abase Himself to take on our humanity, that verily it seemed as his soul had been dragged from his body and were burning like to a furnace. Unable to endure which ardor, he grieved and melted apace, and cried out in a loud voice. And when that measureless fervor came upon him, with it came so sure a hope of his salvation, that he could not in any manner believe that if he were dead he must needs pass through the pains of Purgatory; and this love endured in him full six months, albeit that excessive fervor was not continual, but came upon him at certain hours of the day. And at this time he did receive marvelous visitations of God. He was one night so mightily exalted and rapt in God that he saw in Him the Creator of all things both celestial and terrestrial. And then he knew clearly how every created thing looketh in the eye of its Creator, and how Our Lord is above, and within, and without, and beneath all created things. He also saw and knew one God in three Persons, and three Persons in one God, and the infinite loving-kindness which did make the Son of God incarnate through obedience to the Father. And lastly and finally, he knew in that vision how that there is no other way by which the Soul can journey to God and have Eternal Life, save only through Christ the Blessed, which is the Way and the Truth and the Life of the Soul.

Chapter Twenty-five

OF THAT HOLY MONK TO WHOM THE MOTHER
OF CHRIST APPEARED WHEN HE WAS INFIRM,
AND BROUGHT HIM THREE BOXES OF ELECTUARY.

IN THE aforesaid Convent of Soffiano there
was a Gray Friar of such sanctity that he
seemed all divine, and ofttimes was he rapt in
God. This Brother being on a certain time absorbed in God, forasmuch as he was notably
endowed with the grace of contemplation, there
came unto him birds of divers kinds, and famil-
iarly alighted upon his shoulders, upon his head,
and upon his arms, and marvelously did they
sing. This man was a solitary soul and but rarely spake; but when he was questioned, he made
answer so graciously that he seemed rather an
angel than a man; and he was most fervent in
contemplation; and the Brothers held him in
great reverence. This Brother having fulfilled
the course of his virtuous life, he fell ill even
unto death. All his faith he put in the Heavenly
Physician, Jesus Christ the Blessed, and in His
Blessed Mother; thereby he merited the divine
clemency of being mercifully visited and healed.
Hence he being once in his bed and making
ready for death with all his heart, there appeared unto him the glorious Virgin Mary,
with a great multitude of angels. She drew nigh
unto his bed: whence he was greatly comforted

both in soul and in body; and he began to pray
that She would pray Her beloved Son that
through His merits He would release him from
the prison-house of this wretched flesh. And
persevering in this prayer with many tears, the
Virgin Mary replied to him, calling him by
name, and saying: "Doubt not, son, forasmuch
as your prayer is granted, and I am come to
comfort you a little before that you depart
hence from this life." There were with the Virgin Mary three Holy Virgins, which bore in
their hands three boxes of Electuary of match-
less odor and sweetness. Then the glorious Virgin took and opened one of those boxes; and
taking a small portion of that Electuary in a
spoon, She gave it to the sick man: who felt
such great comfort and ease that it seemed as
his soul could no longer abide within his body;
whence he began so say: "No more, O most
holy and blessed Virgin Mother, no more! for I
am unable to endure such sweetness." But the
pious and benign Mother still offering that Electuary to the sick man and constraining him to
take it, emptied all that box. Then the beatific
Virgin took the second and laid the spoon therein to give to him; whereat he did lament, saying: "O most blessed Mother of God! my soul
is almost melted away by the strength and
sweetness of the first Electuary." The glorious
Virgin Mary answered: "Taste, my son, but a

little of this second box." And giving him a
little, she said: "Now, son, you have so much
as may suffice; be comforted, O son, for I will
come for you ere long, and will lead you to the
kingdom of my Son, which you have ever
sought and desired." And She departed thence;

and he was left so consoled by the sweetness of
that confection, that for several days more he
survived sated and strong, and partaking of no
bodily food. And after some days, joyously discoursing with the Brethren, with great rejoicing, he passed away from this miserable life.